WANDERING

poems by
GEORGIA SAN LI

FINISHING LINE PRESS
Georgetown, Kentucky

WANDERING

Always, For JKJ

ACKNOWLEDGMENTS

To the editors of the following journals where poems in this chapbook first appeared, sometimes with variations:

The Big Bang—*California Quarterly*
Container—*LIT* magazine
We Eat Ugly Lionfish, Americana—*Willow Springs*
Trumpet Sounds—*Atlanta Review*
Wandering—Fauxmoir Lit Mag
Untitled Jazz—*The Antigonish Review*
Remember, In this scroll of paper—*Slow Lightning Anthology*
Unnamed Desire, Determination—*Blackbox Manifold* (UK)
The exodus of young men—selected for the 2023 Oxford Poetry prize shortlist
(November 2023); first published by *The Missouri Review*
The Years—*SWWIM*
The Signifiers—*La Piccioletta Barca*
Forkprints—*Cathexis Northwest Press*

Publisher: Leah Huete de Maines
Editor: Christen Kincaid
Cover Art: "Summer Moon" 2016, linocut print by William H. Hays
Author Photo: Nancy Carbonaro
Cover Design: Elizabeth Maines McCleavy

Order online: www.finishinglinepress.com
also available on amazon.com

Author inquiries and mail orders:
Finishing Line Press
PO Box 1626
Georgetown, Kentucky 40324
USA

Contents

PART I—DREAM-MAKING

The Big Bang
After Jean-Luc Godard

Looking down I stare
      at the circle of roast coffee, languid and hot,
    held neatly by a blue cup and saucer like the dark noisy world
          in orbit, the sultry crème afloat,
like ribbons moving in the current
        growing hotter in condensation
and the chemistry of matter
          rattling with a spoon as a warning
to myself of the limits of language,
        chasing crème to shore
    disappearing to the perimeter
          beyond the edges of the earth—
            my lonesome island bubbles, popping bubbles

I glance sideways at my temptress who watches me from behind,
        and turn, dragging long on my cigarette, like dark noise in
a clear channel,
      warning of the outer orbits
          of my invisible storm, and slowly I finish it—
every resistant black drop—
        before the starry ash of my fingers crumbles

Temptress

We entered the canopy of sycamore wearing
greens of apple, where cinnamon stirred me
and my musings along the campus pathway, and her
sweater draped over her shoulders as

her skirt swayed, brushing against my knee like a
pendulum, waiting for my classes to be done,
ding-dong bells ringing when she would demure and kiss
the soft ice cream cone at the student union,

watching squirrels hoarding acorns in their cheeks
as I squinted through puffs of smoke at papers
left to read at night, sliding them into my leather
satchel, latching the buckles saying, "Let's go," and she

permitted me to take her hand, finishing
her vanilla, biting the wafer with fine porcelain teeth
as I led her to the observatory dome to
look through the full distance of the future, to

where we were going, where I would succumb to
intoxication, the sultry taste of the earth in
my mouth, where I lost all sense of outer space.

Container

Peckish, she pecks to find Beauty
        her Romanesque nose
        her Helen
        infusing her with her soul
        her long-fingered hands of clay, her hips in
such grinding agony, endured
to form and wrench his children,
with her power of catastrophe over
        that object
        that creature
        that enemy
        that human life
containing the workings of
her organs
her plasma
her monster
the umbilical cord of
        her two daughters, then
        her son, severed,
        her duty done,
still hungering, Beauty stays, unsatisfied,
full of wont and bitter accusations

Ambition

constrains us, in paradoxical bindings
and limits of asymptotic lines that
never touch the minimum or
maximum, sliding along quadratic slopes—
we are stuck pinging the Q, the Q, the Q
like Professor Ramsey, until at last, we row
to the Lighthouse again,
firing our arrows high, hearts beating into forbidden dark,
in wanton, unremitting belief that, in due course, life
shall veer into forbidden light

We Eat Ugly Lionfish, circa 1950

I am a pencil
sharpened, searching with my nose,
sparingly whittling away orange wood chips
with a paring knife, as if I were an apple made of wood,
the kindling bunched and crowded like sticks
for refuge in a shed
listening to black boots of war outside
I shiver like a worm in mud
with my brothers, my sisters,
our broken branches—a warm trickle runs over my freezing arm
and we walk again in order of birth
toward the southern light, the day sorting overhead
until we reach the coarse sand and eat ugly lionfish
until we recite our names and history
until we write in the sand and sing about the full moon as
we sit under it
finding a sheet of paper on which to write,
to tear at with my teeth.

Again, Desire
After John Milton, Sonnet 19

This moment is like the last one, concerned with
making good use of itself.
It hears sleet, but does not listen, dashing itself into
the gusto of delight,
letting you see her lips kiss this dark world with
love songs over the scratchings of this sharp
pencil. And still half of
the wretched moment wants to be noticed,
whisking its array of fluorescent tailfeathers,
which it knows without
looking may become strange in this
exposé, its soft bare shoulder making
an appearance from a
velvet gown precisely because
it is both aged and blossoming, making good use
of itself when it considers how its light
is spent in reach for its acts of revision,
the consecrated underbelly
of all this defiant dancing, refusing to wait—

PART II—DEATH SEQUENCE

Trumpet Sounds

In my old age, wearing my
floppy hat to meet the sun
for another moment to walk to
the mailbox, sip an espresso at the café—
      o-la-la! life!—I buy a bag of sumo oranges,
      a farewell gift for my childhood friend from Seoul,
      for who knows if I ever see him again?
I take the longer route home
through the park over
unpaved trails for pull ups and stretches
where dogs bark behind the bungalows called
Barcelona and the latter-day saints
erected a temple, and Saint Gabriel sounds his
trumpet, so soon I reach the intersection
where I decide which way to go
on Palmilla Drive, under the golden air, the tap-tap of
my walking sticks, turning right toward the
pillars holding up the canyon for
      another day of luck, and
            sidestepping the snails

Wandering

During these endless days, I live my life
in the family room where I wake in cosmic
stillness on the narrow bed. It is cool in

the night and from this new dwelling,
I can still see the orientation of the world,
sense the constellations slowly ascending—

leaving their silvery veil over a clay canyon
along the road to the house. I am warm in
my mind's earthly reverie, traversing the river

of mountain snow where I play with my
brothers when we are young boys, where, in its
shallow edges, crayfish swirl up a mix of

rounded pebbles and feathery dust plumes
of magic. I dream vividly, navigating my
sailboat over meadows of memory

at will and slowing my breath to linger
in this space, my imagination firing.
The river beckons to us as an escape—

its uneven motion of danger
and wonder and life. In this meadow,
I am a visitor reaching far back to see

myself and my lost brothers as we were
once upon a time, this fairy tale part of
our inheritance, its quality of golden light,

the taste of meadow grass floating in the
air. The river rock prickles the tender skin
of our bare feet as we splash and plunge

our hands into the mirror, spearing
crayfish hiding in the riverbeds. Our catches
dangling in the air under moonlight—

their dancing desperation makes me
laugh, taste salts, slippery granules of meat.
See my brothers leap along rocky beaches

through the warm salty sprays, the waves
washing our feet! The summer moon rises
across the horizon, marking out its domain.

Together we crouch under its wide light,
digging—

Lost Time

In old age, Death does not bring
suspicions to the mind,
hidden in inevitability, where every new flit—
a keystroke of emotion—
is a happenstance of luck.

What problem is there to solve in such age?
Under the power of his whole life,
in all its respectable imperfections,
Death yielding, as if time were his just reward.

So, how, not why, is he no longer here
to collect it, one moment more of life?
Her thievery, her blockade—
did she stand there, arms akimbo?

Sleepless

*"With the landless gull, that at sunset folds her wings
and is rocked to sleep between billows; so at nightfall,
the Nantucketer, out of sight of land, furls his sails,
and lays him to his rest, while under his very pillow
rush herds of walruses and whales…"*
Moby-Dick, by Herman Melville

The old woman rises, lashing
her voice in live wires
annihilating expectations of
duty, of honor, these weighty virtues
now shed as skin of unwanted burdens
better borne by great walruses
and whales, and instead she slants
her gaze like spotlights across
the bow, jolting unsuspecting
whole bodies of fish out of the sea into
flight under the long purple stone
silhouette of Catalina.

The old woman rises, savagely
leviathan, a daughter of
Poseidon, shearing the stern
with confidence and defiant desire,
knotting her belly, she levels
her decibels, confronting small
horrified faces, turning east,
skimming the sea on hapless wings.

Lost

The family room patio door
squawks open, this sound of
hungry seagulls in a wedge of light
catches tiny sparkles along carpet,
creamy sea foam rolling in with the tides.

You notice a small spider stumbling
over a ledge, a deep footprint
of a bedpost. Its silk threads
flutter like antennae searching for the
bed where it used to be.

Until a gust of late morning smells
of buttered toast and egg he used to
love with coffee, laundry detergent,
the smell of yellow green, reignite a
sense of existence.

Outdoors a spray of red
marigolds stands along the embankment,
as if a scattered memory: two men
hoisting the bed by its handles,
carrying it out like a coffin.

When suddenly, oh, small spider, you
float away like a hot air balloon
without its ballasts, buffeted wildly,
over the lampstand, caught by the hook of
a book light, her sleek long
curve of wiring, your cobwebs spun into
a silvery necklace—

Do her eyes like a lighthouse spot porpoise
leaping in the tumult? Do you follow
the Pequod into another universe aglow
with herds of walruses and whales
rushing beneath your pillow?

What mysteries will overtake you in
the fragility of life? Oh, small spider,
where will you land again like a pin drop
on your delicate feet? When will you
escape from your ghosts?

Untitled Jazz

"In the very essence of poetry there is something indecent:
a thing is brought forth which we didn't know we had in us...."
Ars Poetica? by Czesław Miłosz

I rendered myself tedious, practicing
to dance in the language of jazz,
tilting my diction, and abandoning yesterday's
toast and cherry jam
to enter a pitchy darkness, occupy
and dance blindly in the jungle, seize
its lizards and armadillos and owls,
step on their pretty yellow claws,
lure in their yellow eyes and
change their bored faces scoffing at the band
of birds of paradise, beaks screeching
along trombones, printed music for tourists who bask in the
wild animal park, watching through telescope lenses to catch
a piece of tuille for their box of ephemera,
   where they later close the sash over their lovers, white bristles
      over gray bodies, sex resting in soft silvery fur
which an old woman cleaned as if it were a thistle,
         snapping her sharp tongue before
   tossing it, limpid, along the tough wrought meridian
of overgrown cacti along 163 S to Baja
         blowing seeds of serenity into the wind to plant the bottom
of the Earth, her needles long enough to spear the passing creature,
   firing until she knew, like my mother,
            she had pierced the heart

PART III—FLOOD WATERS

Remember

Do you pray with your eyes open?
  She asks silent questions watching
  her mother's vagaries, part shadow, part light

When do you pray if not when
  your beloved has collapsed, and cancer
  has come to take his life?

When do you pray if not when
  the curtain is pulled open, and you look up
  from a chair at the far side of the room?

When do you pray if not when
  the grown children hold on
  to his hands and weep?

When do you pray if not when
  the grandchildren stand next to the podium
  as the organ pipes play?

When do you pray if not when
  your eyes open, and with curled finger you point at the body,
  his vows fulfilled, till death do you part.

Her mother turns to the blue ashes: Remember—
  When did you pray if not when
  wearing your boutonniere of gardenias at the altar?

Americana on Oak Tree Drive

"…where are the angels I ask That's
just the city's name she says"
Los Ángeles, by Cintia Santana

Charlie Brown, *I waited for you!* my
little sister Sally cried before I cared
that I was a big brother enough to
be bossy, who left her crying
under the school flagpole
because our mother arrived late
walking from our ranch house on
Oak Tree Drive in plastic green
sandals with heels made of cork that
could float like a bottle over the ocean
but ruined her feet, because I waited
for her, too, standing on the yellow
paint lines watching new friends play
tetherball, as round as my head, hitting it
hard, wrapping rope around a metal pipe.
It is 1969 when we rode in the backseat
of my father's Dodge Valiant, no more
summers swum in Pine Lake eating
peanut butter and jam soaked in Wonder
bread in the rain. Gold-rim glasses framed
my sister's face reading *Harriet the Spy*
in the closet for privacy while I organized
a battalion of army men the color of
my mother's sandals with David P. and
David F. sliding on our bellies arranging
make-believe war at eye-level in our backyard
where a swimming pool could fit.
My father used to grow tomatoes and
zucchini for spaghetti he taught our mother
to make from a Betty Crocker cookbook,
which she read mostly guessing because
she did not speak English. It was the year
Nixon is elected President and man
walks on the Moon, Walter Cronkite
reporting, "That's the way it is."
Our parents hosted weekend dinner
parties. She made egg cream puffs stuffed
with Cool Whip craving mochi whet with

red bean paste her mother's housekeeper
made. *왜 왔어*? *Wei- whats-uh? she asked. Why
come this far?* When our father asked why
four bedrooms are not enough, she cited
scripture, *your children are raised by a wife more
precious than rubies.* We saw Lucy and Linus at
reunions, our parents moved to a bigger
house after we left for college, were still
married forty-five years later when states
struck down bans on gay marriage, over 200
countries committed to reduce use of fossil
fuels to preserve the Earth. That spring our
father smiles like an astronaut through
bubbled glass, *또 왔어*? *Tto-whats-uh? You came
again?* His eyes shine as he set down his
briefcase at the front door, his day of work
done, his hand squeezing mine once. I answer
with twice, signaling he is entering the
rooms of my childhood holding my hand
because I had nothing to fear: he is home,
our mother's mouth agape, believing she
had always done what was right. She had
given him everything, made spaghetti out of
nothing, and Sally and I sit crying.

Righteousness

Write your thank you cards for mourners
who came for my father with *jeong*
in their heart? You, murderess widow,
your majesty. What would You otherwise

have to say to me? Still ringing those
falsetto bells in language made of porcupine
quills that quell your throat into silent
nothing that I don't want to speak

in your stead, only to leave me choking
on your kingdoms, your dynasties of
hieroglyphics, of painted caves, your
works of art, annihilating the persimmon

at the peak of harvest time, your horsehair
brush smearing soot over its bleak
autumnal heart, his dark
lady's cheek—that lonely beggar outcast

on the street, she is You that I see, who
refused to let his brother, like Alyosha,
come kiss his cheek! That beggar,
now deadening after years in silence still

breathing soot and smoke of condemnation
she is You—she is Me.

Rank Fruits & Lamentations

a banana peeled open,
its skin rolled into a paper coffee cup,

left with smudges of red lipstick
biting across the lid for a taste of apple,

shelves of epiphany in
library books, a wall of worlds, of

Thou(s)—Who art Thou(s)? Who art We(s)
with crinkled spines for those who live long enough

to stand by the lonely fruit stand laying claim to its
secret road behind a wall of empty carboard

boxes holding forgotten oranges
for those still hunting, snarling bellies

on the street after midnight,
the new day approaching,

in front of the psychedelic van, the driver's
window open to let the night air through,

new summer peaches and blushing pears
arranged to face the soggy dawn,

soaking in oils and rot of what these fruits will
become, kicked, and melted into the curb

of the tarry pit of our post-historic times—
dissolving, stinking with the last of the onions

Depletion

breakage, slurries of writing in runoff—
are bells of the chapel ringing?

ding-dong. Whose squeaking chair
and desk's far corner, whose sheaf of

papers catch aphorisms, clichés,
cartoons and purple metaphors,

strumming to shake loose a minstrel's
twang against her thumb and fingers,

thrumming, using her re-sharpened lead,
a blade to ooze open the taut heart,

already broken, chaos splashed against blank
pages, dripping yellow, green; write with

blunted tip as though the subject were
dead and drawn in memoriam, softly

At the airport

a slash of pink neon light
breaks across the pillars at Not Your

Average Joe's next to the United
counter, while we wait at

gate B and move away through
our earbuds as we tune out one-sided

conversations spiking out above the
clinking glasses in time and place

out into canals of other unheard voices, while
pointing, directing fellow humanity to follow signs

down the corridors, wait for their
arrivals, their departures, as we wait for

signs of acknowledgement in—
this small, small

disconnected world—
waiting in the air of masks,

each of us alone and surrounded,
waiting, to enter somewhere else

Unnamed Desire

After Bob Dylan, A Hard Rain's a-Gonna Fall

A hard rain is rising and
falling in this cavern, where
my drip-drip face assembles
itself from stalagmite into
a mask of my father as if
marking itself again so that he
would recognize me as his
offspring in the wilderness
where I have summoned
with all my might what
I hoped was sufficient ingenuity
and determination
so that there would be a medal
to bring back across the silver
lake by ferry from
Chuncheon City—is that you
singing, father, in the sound of
voices at my bedside
strumming a bipa
so that I follow it
home again where you've
been longing to see me: *but
don't come before the
time comes, not before a
good long life*: but see this
form? I am ready, empty-
handed. Is that your
foghorn calling out to me,
rolling open the stone at my
voice box? I hear
that ballad you are singing for
me father, I can hear you asking
where have you been, what
have you seen and heard, who
did you meet, what
have you done,
and as I come closer, I hear you
asking: *why son, have your
eyes turned from my starry black
to blue?* Can you hear
me, father? I am singing.

PART IV—EARTH & GRAVITY

Untitled: a portrait from the tarmac

Take down your dancing shoes
slip them on your youthful mind
looking up into the sunset, empty

skies filling your eyes with vision
No one walks along the road of life
with you now, so, you whistle an

old folksong talking to that stranger
you remember, who, when you landed
at Chicago O'Hare on that Pan Am

flight in 1964, emerged from the crowd
after waiting behind the chain-linked
fence—now a noble creature,

re-render the marble torso under his
white button-down dress shirt, the stroke
of a brow line, from the side, his

handsome earlobe, his shining black hair
whisked by the windy city. You play
with this fire, yank at your throbbing heart,

no longer a stranger, now that these
skies are empty though this ambition and
hopes are still tangling and burn

into knots—but at least now let us
dance, let me call you *dahngshin*, let me
see you forever in front of my eyes

> *"…Admit it, and your house will fall to ruin;*
> *refuse it, and your story ends."*
> A Cry Over Water by Nan Cohen

The exodus of young men
from South Korea / after the war / second sons like my father / from
yangban houses / who fulfilled their military duties / then left for
America / for their futures / with their intellects / with ambitions and
philosophies of life / they chose from the choices they had / and he /
chose to start his family / at Eagle Heights / not far from my birthplace
not far from University Hospital / where I have returned / to my future
my American heartland / in a white rental / white / the Korean color
of grief / it is more visible in hazardous skies / and now I remember /
how he loved to fish in these lakes / and I imagine schools of perch /
swimming / to old Bayside for hundreds of years / amid spotted cows /
harkening home to the canton of Glarus, / once Ennenda / Netstal and
Riedern / schools of perch /their whirring clasped under my ribs / as
if caged in the Earth / in its heavy / aged ice / I grip the wheel quaking
/ holding my yearning for the ocean / in great swells / suddenly / they
flood my limbs / pinch my feet and ankles / swollen with generations
past / whom my father brought over oceans in exodus / the inevitable
reformation along wild grasses / fields of corn and barley /where warm
chestnut trees once stood in dusk like this

listening for history / poetry / and literature / in memories of my father
along pastures and traces / whirring quietly / whirring home / to this
land amid cherry orchards and milk

Ode to Hans Castorp

our orchestral transit on
the New World Symphony of trains
enters the tunnel to the magic mountain of
Hans Castorp, gasping with consumption,
he fights for purity
hewing to his rest cure of icy air,
climbing out of fever for Lady Chauchat,
listening for her clanging doors, grand entrances
into the cafeteria to dine with gloves and waltz
along a lyrical din of bassoons
and trumpets of sciences and war,
gathering his peaks of love and honor
he fights through the muddy doom,
climbing for all chances
to lead this treacherous life

To love the earth

and wear its thick coat of
winter, its frosty courage
borne by its Achilles heel of love

to lean on in shaping the emptiness
from a strong footing against
the ice floes breaking apart

over an egg harbor safeguarding
the schools of perch learning to
speak, their little mouths mimicking

their mothers, writing songs in
perfumes of the invisible water until
spring ushers them into inlets and

scrawls of the rivers to finally wrest
fifty years from bended knee

The Years

when I turn over the cards of
   time I am passing blurry sheep
along the Autobahn the sun

blinding my eyes with silver
   sheen the pavement ahead
seems matter of fact and dry

disarray a long documentary
   no decorations no earrings on
small ears no sweet rainbow

lifesavers no snow no vixen in blue
   berry patches no
holly prickles no upright

piano for books of etudes
   to practice to someday play
the Italian Concerto wrapped

in brown paper years after
   dolls with hair washed with
toothpaste and ruined I crawl

under the coffee table already
   abandoned to find myself
restless to collect warmth and

kisses on my many dappled faces
   on our way to Wilhelmshaven—
there to the cold Black Sea

PART V—RE-MEMORY MATERIAL & TIME

The Signifiers

Do birds in the new world cityscape
know time, and existence,
when grasping bits of
straw grass from
cracks of cement,
or mulching, for nesting in spindly
trees excavated from nature, made
neat, their roots wrapped in burlap
bandages, torn away from motherlands,
where distant armies stand
over rocks and dead bodies?
It is time to stop the threads that
you have intercepted like lightning
bugs, biting your ankles, in combat
for peace in the forgetting, cupped
like a last drink of water in your hands,
their wings clipped, yet slashing
the lines in your palms,
changing the fates and the promises
that have come undone as you poured over
scenes that must have happened at nighttime
when it was just the two of you, parents in the
magnified light I want to let go but can't,
holding you tight, here in the dark.

Soon

Soon the impervious rays peek over her pillow
        waking delicate dew, clinging to greens uncurling

Soon silver canopies sing from the pews planted along the
        road someone made leaving the village

Soon she leans on the tips of her toes to
        wave goodbye to the children,

Soon she yanks at her roots, ensnaring her
        uncanny silver rabbit

Soon thawing, thawing, the moon,
        its heavenly limelight rising too late to open her eyes

Forkpoints

pressed against copper reveal
patterns of fossilized flowers mixed with

mud-cracked seeds, pebbling rocks
of brown barley, red beans, smashed

leaving imprints against char-riddled
rice, scraped and singed at the bottom of her

pan, panning gold, but *aiyishii*
there is nothing, nothing

burning bright in the cruel bubbling rivers of
indelible summer heat she slurps before

she sets the table, and knows not what to call this
American alien mixture of no lilacs, no

tubers, with no redemption in
their eyes

Epitome, *He*

From 30000 feet outside an
icy double pane the rocky
mountain ridges could and
would distort their shape, strewn

into a tray of daily bread, the
warm-crusted tartines, nothing
fancy, just as he liked to bite into
with coffee, on what would be

his last trip to Le Jardin des
Jardins, the last long wild violet
dusk splashing the sky, too early
for the scent of lavender, sitting at

Bistrot des Philosophes where
we stop to savor one more cozy
bière pression, invited into
someone's warm kitchen filled with

shelves of books to talk about
whatever freely comes to mind,
stopping time before we resume
whatever will come next—

without him and with him
walking north, there,
on the maddening Moon

Present Location

Often we sit at day 7 by
night 7 as if Time were

coordinated into a neat box
situating itself in a corner

of the future as you look
at Time's immovable

hand only pretending to
sleep instead of dreaming

relentlessly of backstory
part memory and

part re-rendering but She is
Now holding you in blue

opacity waiting in dramatic
Shakespearean suspense

until quivering wayward in
involuntarily motion pulling

forward through the unread
reading pile with a blank

handkerchief for tears
kissing Her awake
with wide bursting breaths

In this scroll of paper

let's say in this very moment
we are in dialogue, you
pulling me up with rope from my
churning chest, my stiff cold fingertips
slowly playing piano in the air to
reach your voice, your words
with you conjured in my mind,
my consciousness and yours
overlapping in our worlds of
imagination in this space

what will I write if I live to next year
or let's set another decade as the
intention of our ambition to live,
let's be optimistic, let's say, you and
I will meet again as old friends and
until then let's live with that hope,
repeating ourselves from the beginnings
again, and again, for an encore that signifies
our creation was overall—long or short—
in service, like the young Queen's, and
worth the while.

Determination

wonders where we shall go
today or tomorrow and we begin
pondering Dr. Pozzi at Home,
in that red *robe de chambre*
on a wall near Madame X on the other side
at the museum as a simulcast in your
memory plays stone shiisaas set outside on the stakes
of a gate by someone who lives inside
Determination made of low
thatch, where shoes have
been arranged to go in and sing
with daughters and sons and play
an old banjo, throw rings to catch
one of the pegs, hooray, cheers for
the ringers, and in passing we
note that achieving the
aim is not the aim as Determination smiles
with her grandmother-eyes, her
bare feet dancing, yesterday's empty
plum wine bottle balanced on her
head in a state of mutatis mutandis
sitting across a table as if family
were friends and life easy going with
Determination to straighten
bending bones, plying anguish into
legumes and purple tubers pulled from
the devastation and Determination to
find food after tornados, sufficient
nutriments to keep gardening for
a few hours a day, tend the cabbage
and cucumber vines in
the late light of autumn before we
return to Mozart for whimsy
though there are root systems of
sorrowful joy in poetry
that cannot be helped.

Traces

the splash of
freckled
sun glitters on

his cheeks,
imprints of its
heavenly kisses,

her lipstick, lonely
under
star-cut prisms

of sky light
glowing
over cherry

wood, like ashy
petals,
meaningless money,

mere sheafs of
paper, twisted
pages, half

written,
half uttered,
fueling a

bit of bone and
blood against the
frost of time and

memory—catch these
falling laces,
before they melt,

such crystal
beauty—
this snowfall

With Gratitude

to my marvelous teachers for their dedication to teaching: Nan Cohen, Peggy Dobreer, Janet Fitch, Anna Freeman, Elizabeth Gaffney, Dave King, Thomas McNeely, Nami Mun, and the late Nancy Zafris.

to this fellowship of poets and writers: Mauro Altamura, Arleen Armstrong, Miki Armstrong, Judith Blak, Jason Lee Braun, Ruby Carlson, Christy Chung, Janet Clare, Vivian Clausing, Geoff Cohen, Alicia Dekker, Jenny Devlin, Kim Elliott, Elizabeth England, Lisa Estus, Brittany Gibbons, Hannah Heller, Mary Hester, Sadie Horton, Jacinta Camacho Kaplan, Anu Krishnaswamy, Stephanie Mankins, Lori Mann, Diane Masucci, Sara Mauer, Samuel Mireles, Carrie Nassif, Cynthia Nooney, Jamie O' Halloran, David Orr, Carol Parchewsky, Amy Parish, Glenna Penner, Jasper Rine, Jim Roberts, Emily Rubin, Rebecca Rudy, Katrina Ryan, Mike Saeugling, Jonathan Sapers, June Stoddard, Vivian Wang, Jane Wieder, Nancy Williard, Rachel Wineberg, Marion Wyce, and Carol Zapata-Whelan.

to Sandra Brooks, Carolyn Callahan, Rebecca Cressman, Anne W. Crowley, Stefanie Dangermond, Amy Gray, Amy Hill, Patricia Hillman, Hannah Kim, Lisa Mitrovich, Michelle Olson, Eileen Pyne, Athena Sarantinos, Renee Schor, Sara Sun, Harriet Wingard and Millicent Yim, for defining the treasures of friendship.

to the Community of Writers at Olympic Valley, Slow Lightning Poetry, and the Kenyon Review Workshops in poetry and fiction.

*

In loving memory of my paternal grandmother
Kae Soon Lee—May 4, 1910–June 28, 1989
816 Geuhm San Li (village), Gahng Won Do (province), South Korea

GEORGIA SAN LI is currently at work on poetry and *Untitled: a portrait from the tarmac*, a novel. She has worked on extended assignments in cities including Tokyo, Tunis, Paris, London, Mexico City, Sao Paulo, Denver, and Wilhelmshaven. She currently lives and works in New England. She was shortlisted for the 2023 Oxford Poetry Prize and her recent work appears or is forthcoming in *Blackbox Manifold* (UK), *The Glacier, Osmosis Press* (UK), *LIT Magazine,* and *The Missouri Review.*

www.ingramcontent.com/pod-product-compliance
Lightning Source LLC
Chambersburg PA
CBHW020222090426
42734CB00008B/1182